C000144043

# ANGLESEY

## The Island's Story
*By Michael Senior*

Printed and published by:
Gwasg Carreg Gwalch,
Iard yr Orsaf, Llanrwst, Gwynedd. LL26 0EH
☎ (01492) 642031    Fax: (01492) 641502

ISBN: 0-86381-389-5

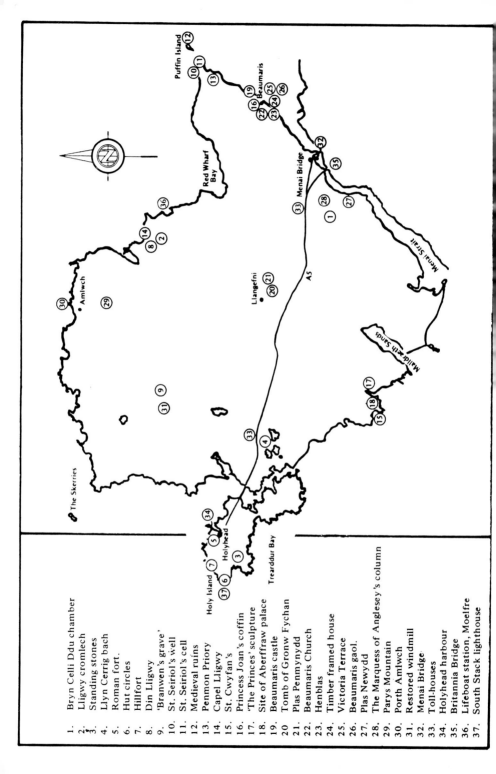

1. Bryn Celli Ddu chamber
2. Lligwy cromlech
3. Standing stones
4. Llyn Cerrig bach
5. Roman fort.
6. Hut circles
7. Hillfort
8. Din Lligwy
9. 'Branwen's grave'
10. St. Seiriol's well
11. St. Seiriol's cell
12. Medieval ruins
13. Penmon Priory
14. Capel Lligwy
15. St. Cwyfan's
16. Princess Joan's coffin
17. 'The Princes' sculpture
18. Site of Aberffraw palace
19. Beaumaris castle
20. Tomb of Gronw Fychan
21. Plas Penmynydd
22. Beaumaris Church
23. Henblas
24. Timber framed house
25. Victoria Terrace
26. Beaumaris gaol.
27. Plas Newydd
28. The Marquess of Anglesey's column
29. Parys Mountain
30. Porth Amlwch
31. Restored windmill
32. Menai Bridge
33. Toll-houses
34. Holyhead harbour
35. Britannia Bridge
36. Lifeboat station, Moelfre
37. South Stack lighthouse

# Preface to the Revised Edition

For a time a Borough within the county of Gwynedd, the island's identity remains secure as it now regains its older county status. It would be easy for an independent-minded island to stagnate, but this has never been Anglesey's habit. Its history is full of movement, of coming and going, and it is symbolically appropriate that one of the most striking innovations, since I first wrote this book, is the highly modern, not to say modernistic, new terminal at Holyhead.

What is perhaps more surprising is that as Anglesey launches itself forward towards the next millennium with such up-to-date facilities, at the same time its past expands as well. There is, for instance, now an increasing understanding of the role the island played in the period of the independent princes, as provided by the work recently carried out at Llanfaes and Newborough by the Gwynedd Archeological Trust.

It is heartening to find as well that steadily increasing visitor numbers testify to the value of the island's history to the modern traveller. While many may come for its beaches, caravan camps, and its high-quality attractions such as the Sea Zoo, it is clear from the figures that many more people now enjoy the experience of getting a glimpse into history, as at Plas Newydd or Llynon Mill.

Sometimes when I see the cars and caravans flooding westwards along the new A55 I fear that the island may be sinking beneath this weight of attention. But here as elsewhere the intensity of this pressure is restricted to certain times of year. For much of the time the island has a great deal to offer the discerning visitor, particularly those enticed by depths of history.

*Michael Senior,*
*Glan Conwy, January 1996*

# A PLACE OF ANCIENT HABITATION

NGLESEY is essentially a part of the coastal plain which stretches westwards from the Snowdonia mountains. It became an island in glacial times, when the relative levels of land and sea changed by about 60 feet, and one of Anglesey's many parallel river valleys flooded, forming the Menai Strait. It thus now forms a compact square-shaped piece of level land some 290 square miles in area, 23 miles across diagonally on its longest, south-east to north-west axis.

Geologically it is an old land. Based mainly on pre-Cambrian rock, on which were deposited overlays of shale (such as that forming Parys Mountain) and limestone, still prominent in outcrops such as the headland of Penmon, it bears a certain degree of uniformity. Ice flowing down the Irish Sea stripped the overlays from most areas other than the north, and when the glaciers melted they deposited a topsoil of boulder clay which gives to the island its high fertility. It is this which has led to its relative density of population both in ancient and more recent times and to its many well-established settlements.

Several features have changed, over these thousands of years. The marshiness of the low-lying valleys such as that of the Afon Cefni at Malltraeth is still increasing, caused by the relatively recent building-up of sand drifts near the coast which impede the drainage. Perhaps most radically, the interior of the island has become gradually less wooded. Excavations at archeological sites reveal that this was originally covered with oak and hazel, and it will help us to understand the pattern of the early settlements if we remember that for the first few thousand years of its inhabitation all of Anglesey away from the coast was densely forested.

Anglesey lies at a crucial point in the seaways of western Britain, a fact which has enabled it to benefit from trade and hence from widespread sources of influence. The same fact has equivalently made it vulnerable to invasion. The name itself is testimony to these circumstances, since it is a Norse word borne here by Viking marauders, meaning 'island in the strait'.

In the third millennium B.C., the 'Old Stone Age', a movement of peoples in Europe gave rise to new patterns of settlement. With the concurrent development of farming these migrations stabilised into settled communities with an evident degree of social organisation. These Paleolithic farmers appear

*Bryn Celli Ddu, neolithic burial chamber*

5

*Bryn Celli Ddu, neolithic burial chamber*

*The Lligwy cromlwch*

# A PLACE OF ANCIENT HABITATION

to have arrived in Anglesey during the second half of the third millennium B.C., and it is their work which forms the earliest items in Anglesey's visible history.

The form taken by the evidence for the eventual stability of these settlements is the abundance of megalithic tombs. This type of burial, in a structure known by the Welsh word 'cromlech', spanned a considerable period, probably extending through the later stone age into the beginning of the new culture based on the use of bronze.

There are 20 such monuments left on Anglesey, out of an originally larger number, indicating an evidently relatively dense population during that time. The collection forms probably the largest concentration of monuments for this period in the country. Add to these the slightly later stone circles and standing stones, thought to belong to the period of the so-called 'Beaker' people, the imigrants of the Bronze Age, and we have plenty of evidence for the island's ancient inhabitation.

One of the best preserved chamber tombs in Britain is that known as Bryn Celli Ddu (1), situated not far from the village of Llanddaniel Fab, in the south of the island. Although at first sight a miniature version of the great burial mounds of the Boyne valley in Ireland, it is in fact closer in form to those of Brittany. As it stands now it has as it were been rerofed, its mound being replaced after excavations and clearance in the 1920's. In fact the mound as it is now is not authentic, but must be regarded rather as a protection against further damage, since the whole of the area some 160 feet in diameter marked out by a ditch and outer ring of stones would have been covered by a vast cairn of stones and earth.

The chamber, though clearly the main feature, did not lie at the mound's centre, so that we may surmise that the mound had other functions than that of covering the main burial, and a patterned stone found just outside its closed end may have served some ritual purpose. Within the chamber both cremated and unburnt bones were found, and a remarkable feature of the chamber (which occurs in similar form in other such monuments) is its smoothly-dressed pillar. There were signs of fire and burnt remains also at the centre of the monument, near the patterned stone, where a pit containing fragments of wood and a small piece of burnt human bone was found under the slab known as the central stone.

Unfortunately all we can do is record these facts, and to interpret them would be mere speculation. It seems fair, however, to infer that cremation was practised as part of the ritual connected with these tombs. This is further demonstrated by the detailed modern excavations carried out at Anglesey's

*Standing stones at Penrhos Feilw*

# A PLACE OF ANCIENT HABITATION

other notable cromlech, that known as Barclodiad-y-Gawres, on the west coast between Aberffraw and Rhosneigr. Here both human and animal bones had been burnt, the fragments being purposefully scattered on the chamber's floor.

The chamber tomb of Barclodiad-y-Gawres, as may be seen from old photographs, was a hunched collection of slabs on an exposed promontory, and must have carried a certain romantic atmosphere. In its present state it is unfortunately of no interest to anyone. Covered by a concrete dome, its neatly formal entrance defended by a padlocked grill, its ancient sacredness has been as effectively destroyed as it might have been, left to nature, by storm and thoughtlessness; lovers of antiquity would be wise to stay away.

The name indicates that the passage and chamber were originally covered, not by an earth mound as at present, but by a cairn of small stones. It means 'the giantess' apronful', and derives (as does a cairn of the same name above the Conwy valley) from a folk tale in which a giantess, carrying in her apron a collection of small stones for building, was induced at this spot to let them drop. Early reports indicate that by the early 19th century this cairn had been used to build neighbouring walls.

What is remarkable about Barclodiad-y-Gawres is the extent of the mural art discovered there, a feature which, together with its form, connects it strongly to the Irish tombs of the Boyne valley. It possesses similarities too to instances of such structures in Spain and Portugal, a feature which perhaps indicates the direction of movement during the Stone Age migrations. The decorated stones bear spirals and zig-zags, and together with that at Bryn Celli Ddu they consitute almost the only examples of megalithic art to be found in identifiable British tombs. Only one other case occurs, the 'Calderstones' of Liverpool, and the tomb with which those stones were connected has long ago disappeared.

Of the other monuments of this period the most impressive is the burial chamber at Bodowyr, near Llangaffo, in the southern part of the island not far from Bryn Celli Ddu. Another striking example is the Lligwy burial chamber (2), not far from Din Lligwy, in which the vastness of the capstone indicates a method of construction by undermining rather than raising, and in fact the use of a natural hollow for the chamber makes the whole structure, with its uprights largely below ground level, look somewhat squat.

The standing stones which dot the island extensively, attributed to the Bronze Age people, continue to be a mystery, since it may be assumed that to raise such large slabs into permanent position must have needed the motive of a compelling purpose, and such a purpose is not apparent. Such great uprights as those at Penrhos Feilw (3) appear to proclaim some significance which still eludes us.

# THE END OF
# THE OLD RELIGION

HEN practical purposes seem to be absent, as with the standing stones so abundant in Anglesey, we instinctively attribute a religious motive. In this case we might be right to do so, since it is known from other sources that Anglesey was a major centre of the old religion. 'Druid' is a relatively late and somewhat misleading term, correctly referring to the class of priest or teacher which formed an important part of the social structure of the Celtic tribes during the Roman expansion. There is no reason to suppose, however, that the Druids invented what they taught, and it is therefore possible that the spiritual values which they preached on Anglesey in the early years of this era were those which had been thriving there for thousands of years before they came.

The Celts moved into Britain in about 500 B.C., bringing with them the knowledge of the use of iron. It seems (in spite of the known importance of their priesthood) that they were militaristic people. A famous collection of artefacts found at Llyn Cerrig Bach, three miles south-east of Valley, during the construction of Valley airfield in 1942-3, (4) indicates a high degree of military organisation in the early Iron Age — although of course it might have been an untypical selection due to the circumstances of its disposal.

The Llyn Cerrig Bach find leads to the conclusion that this was a place of ritual offering. It appears from other instances that the Iron Age Celts were in the habit of casting valuable objects into lakes. The finds — which include ornaments and tools, and a large number of animal bones, as well as the swords, spear-heads, parts of chariots and harness which indicate warfare — date from the middle of the second century B.C., and end in the middle of the first century A.D., so that we know we are not dealing with a sudden or accidental loss.

Possibly the quantity and nature of the objects indicate that Anglesey was, during this period, a place of refuge for people from other parts of Britain. The cessation in about A.D. 60 certainly coincides with the arrival of the Romans. We know from written sources quite a lot about that background to this archeological evidence.

Ironically we have a first-hand account of the old religion only at the very moment when it was about to be destroyed. One of the reasons for the Roman invasion of Britain in the first place was that Gaul could not be pacified while

*Iron age find from Llyn Cerrig bach*

11

*Caer Gybi Roman fort*

*Cytiau Gwyddelod, prehistoric hut circles*

# THE END OF THE OLD RELIGION

there was an independent seat of resistance so close; and we may surmise that the religion played a major part in this strength. Julius Caesar tells us that the Druid religion in Europe was 'thought to have been invented in Britain and from there imported into Gaul; even today,' he says, 'those who want to study it in depth normally go to Britain to do so.'

When the Romans under the leadership of Suetonius Paulinus set out to invade Anglesey in A.D. 61 there seems little doubt that the destruction of Druidism was a conscious aim. Tacitus says explicitly that it became necessary 'to attack the island of Anglesey, which was feeding the native resistance.' The other evidence allows us to infer from that that just as Britain was the traditional centre of Druidism for Europe, so Anglesey was for Britain.

Suetonius arrived on the shore of the Menai Strait with a considerable force. Besides two legions, perhaps some 6,000 men, he brought with him 4,000 mercenaries and other additional infantry, together with a troop of cavalry. This formidable army reached the bank opposite Anglesey, and there it stopped. Tacitus in his Annals gives a graphic account, clearly based on an eye-witness view, of what happened next, as they looked across the Strait:

> By the shore stood an opposing battle-line, thick with men and weapons, women running between them, like the Furies in their funeral clothes, their hair flowing, carrying torches; and Druids among them, pouring out frightful curses with their hands raised high to the heavens, our soldiers being so scared by the unfamiliar sight that their limbs were paralysed, and they stood motionless and exposed to be wounded.

The Annals record that the general urged them not to fear a troop of frenzied women, and persuaded them across. In fact we know that the foot-soldiers were ferried over on a flotilla of flat-bottomed boats which had come from Chester, and as the attack was launched at low-tide the horses swam. They felled the Druids where they stood, and burnt their sacred groves. The priests, who preached pacifism, apparently offered no resistance, relying on their gods. Tacitus says that they were 'devoted to cruel superstitions', and that 'they deemed it a duty, indeed, to cover their altars with the blood of captives, and to consult their deities through human entrails.' Although some such cult of human sacrifice cannot of course be ruled out, his account can hardly be taken as unbiased, and other descriptions of Druidism show it to have been a largely pacific and philosophical institution.

Due to the historical accident that Queen Boudicca's rebellion broke out in the south at just that time, Suetonius did not succeed in colonising the island.

*Hillfort on Holyhead Mountain*

*The entrance*

14

# THE END OF THE OLD RELIGION

He had, however, dealt the Druid religion a lethal blow, and some 17 years later his successor Agricola subdued Anglesey more fully.

During much of the Roman period Anglesey would have been controlled from the major fort at Segontium, now Caernarfon. The small Roman fort at Holyhead, which remarkably encloses the present church, dates from a later period, the third to fourth century A.D., when troops had been withdrawn from Segontium and the island was therefore left to defend itself from the increasing coastal raids. (5)

Though that is the only example of Roman work on Anglesey, many of the early native settlements remaining date in their final form from this period. Hut circles such as those on Holyhead Mountain are a form of dwelling which was probably in use over a very long period, being simply the stone bases of round wigwam-like huts made of branches and thatch. Where they have been excavated finds have previously shown them to have been in use in the 2nd, 3rd and 4th centuries A.D., whereas recent investigation of those on Holyhead Mountain dates their use as early as 1500 B.C. (6)

In Anglesey several of these clusters of huts are known by the same name, 'Cytiau Gwyddelod', the Irishmen's huts, and although there is no evidence to suggest that they were in fact the dwellings of Irish invaders it is highly likely that they were in use during the period of prolonged Irish raids, after the partial withdrawal of Roman troops from Segontium in 290 A.D.

From this period too date the ring forts of Din Sylwy, on the eastern promontory of Red Wharf Bay, and the straggling Caer y Tŵr which surrounds the summit of Holyhead Mountain. These are part of a long chain of such fortifications in North Wales, which seem to occupy almost every prominent coastal hilltop.

Din Sylwy, on the hill known as Bwrdd Arthur, 'Arthur's Table', surrounds a wide stretch of remarkably flat table-land in an excellent defensive situation, with steep slopes surrounding its plateau, commanding impressive views over Red Wharf Bay in one direction and Puffin Sound in the other. Since the wall of the hillfort encloses about 17 acres a sizable population is indicated, not only to provide the large workforce needed to construct it but also, presumably, to man such a defensive line of fortifications in time of need. The wall is not now particularly notable, but from what can be seen of it it is clear that it is of the same form as that of Din Lligwy (described below), and finds dating from Roman and sub-Roman times show that it had the same period of use.

The main feature of Caer y Tŵr, on Holyhead Mountain, is its entrance, (7), from which the long breakwater and the harbour of Holyhead can be seen

*The entrance to the main hut at Din Lligwy*

*Din Lligwy, 4th century village*

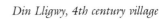

# THE END OF THE OLD RELIGION

below, in almost aerial perspective, emphasising the function of such structures of protection not so much from landward neighbours as from visitations from the sea.

The hut settlements inevitably occurred on the coast, and favoured limestone terraces, because these were places where the tree cover could not establish itself. Because of their position they would be both prepared for and vulnerable to Irish raids. One of the most unusual cases of the remains of a settlement of this time is that known as Din Lligwy, inland from Moelfre, where an earlier open village appears to have been surrounded by a defensive wall in the 4th century A.D., the time of the Roman withdrawal.

Din Lligwy (8) is unusual for structures of this time in having a number of square-built houses, as well as the usual circular ones, and this use of angles indicates the persistance here of Roman influence, which is also strongly suggested by the degree of sophistication with which an otherwise familiar form is here developed.

Its buildings are elaborately constructed of double walls of laid slabs with an infill of loose rubble. The builders used the immediately local limestone slabs and even incorporated limestone outcrops as flooring and as part of the boundary wall. A large round hut at the top end of the site (8), with views out to the sea in two directions, is so finely made as to suggest the dwelling of a chief. It has a beautifully rounded interior wall of dressed stone, a formal entrance involving rising steps, and a spacious air of status almost approaching grandeur. All in all, what we have in Din Lligwy seems likely to be the native Anglesey equivalent of the Roman villa so common elsewhere, a complex homestead based on the dwelling of a person of status.

We shall see in a later chapter how the history of copper mining has influenced the development of Anglesey, but it must be mentioned at this point that there is evidence that copper was already being extracted from Parys Mountain in these Roman and sub-Roman times. This source of wealth may well have been a cause of the extensive habitations and fortifications which stretch in something of a ring around the northern end of the island.

The effects of its inevitable contacts with Ireland, from the megalithic art and tomb-construction of perhaps about 2,500 B.C. through the post-Roman time of the 'Irishmen's huts' must have been significant, and the connection is brought out in the authentic Welsh traditional tale of 'Branwen'. The story tells how the king of Ireland asked for the hand of the daughter of the king of North Wales, and sailed to the royal seat of Aberffraw in Anglesey to take her home. Because of the way she is treated in Ireland, Wales and Ireland go to war, and the slaughter is such that only seven men return with the sad queen to

'Branwen's grave'

# THE END OF THE OLD RELIGION

Anglesey:

> And they came to land at Aber Alaw in Talebolion. And then they sat down and rested. Then she looked on Ireland and on the Island of the Mighty, such as she might see of them. 'Alas, Son of God,' she said, 'that ever I was born! Two good islands have been laid waste because of me!' And she gave a great sigh, and with that her heart broke. They made a four-sided grave for her, and buried her there on the bank of the Alaw.

Sure enough, at the point where the River Alaw flows through the north-west of Anglesey towards Holyhead there is a spot traditionally known as Ynys Branwen, 'Branwen's island', where a burial mound may still be seen. It is known as 'Branwen's Grave', (9) and when it was excavated in 1813 it was found to contain a middle Bronze Age urn in which were some cremated bones. Here the low-lying coast looks directly west towards Ireland, and possibly just after the sun has set one might see the Wicklow Hills (as from several parts of Anglesey's coast) from the top of a rise nearby.

The Irish invasion became such a problem that eventually the people of Gwynedd sent for help from their compatriots in northern England, and a fighting force came south from the area of Hadrian's Wall, somewhere around the year 400.

This was a significant event for Wales and Britain, since it established in this part of North Wales the most powerful dynasty which the native population was ever to possess, that of the house of Gwynedd which eventually gave rise to the independent Welsh princes. In due course a conclusive battle took place in Anglesey which rid Wales of the Irish and established there one of the seats of this royal line. The tale of Branwen indicated that the court at Aberffraw dates from a very early period, and it may well have been founded then.

# THE COMING
# OF CHRISTIANITY

**T**HE king who inherited the new stable situation in North Wales after the expulsion of the Irish from Anglesey was Maelgwn Gwynedd, who had his main seat at Deganwy overlooking the Conwy river. A man of energy and enthusiasm, he exerted his power as a Christian ruler by the foundation of a number of monasteries. One of these was that given to St Cybi at Holyhead, at the site of the Roman fort already referred to, in the year 540 A.D. At the same time monastic lands were provided for his colleague St Seiriol at Penmon.

These 'saints' were evangelical monks who travelled down the western coast of Britain during the sixth century, probably drawing their inspiration from St Columba's religious centre of Iona. At Penmon now we may see the magnificent long-term results of St Seiriol's presence there, and even some contemporary evidence of his first simple foundation, in the form of the well (10) in which he baptised his converts and the outline of the cell (11) in which he very probably lived.

It seems that Seiriol also founded the monastic settlement on the nearby island, now known as Puffin Island, formerly called after him Ynys Seiriol, and also significantly known by the Norse name of Priestholm. There he was buried, and perhaps also his patron King Maelgwn. All that remains there now is the tower of a 12th century church, and the ruins of monastic buildings of that period, (12), with signs of older structure incorporated. It is known that the community there descended from Seiriol's ancient original transposed itself to the mainland, to amalgamate with Penmon, in 1237. It was at that time that the latter underwent considerable rebuilding.

Puffin Island entered history when King Cadwallon, a descendant of Maelgwn, was besieged there by Edwin of Northumbria, in A.D. 632, perhaps one of the first signs of the expansion of the new Anglo-Saxon kingdoms. Indeed no less a person that the 8th century historian Bede records that it was Edwin who brought the islands of Anglesey and Man ('the southern island is the larger and more fertile') under English rule. Puffin Island remained from its early days a vulnerable but populous hermitage, being described by Giraldus Cambrensis — 'Gerald the Welshman', an adventurous cleric who accompanied Archbishop Baldwin on a journey through Wales in 1188, and much to our good fortune recorded his impressions. It is, he says,

*St Seiriol's well, at Penmon*

*St Seiriol's cell*

*Medieval ruins on Puffin Island*

22

# THE COMING OF CHRISTIANITY

known as 'the ecclesiastical island, because many bodies of saints are deposited there, and no woman is suffered to enter it.'

> There is a small island, almost adjoining to Anglesey, which is inhabited by hermits, living by manual labour and serving God. It is remarkable that when, by the influence of human passions, any discord arises among them, all their provisions are devoured and infested by a species of small mice, with which the island abounds; but when the discord ceases they are no longer molested . . .

What we see at Penmon Priory (13) now is partly the remains of domestic monastic buildings of the 13th century. The dovecote, dating from 1600, with its magnificently sturdy corbelled roof, is rightly famous. At the back of the complex lies the Priory Church, the nave being the earliest part, of around 1140, with transcepts dating from some 20 years later. The chancel was originally built in the 13th century, but has been rebuilt twice, once in the 15th century and again in 1855.

There is less evidence now for Cybi's heritage than there is for Seiriol's, the parish church which occupies his site being mainly of the 15th and 16th centuries. The two contemporary saints undoubtedly had a permanent influence of Anglesey, however, beyond the buildings to which they gave rise. They ensured that Anglesey would be a place of many early churches. Indeed the earliness of Christianity's establishment all over Anglesey is attested by a multitude of inscriptions, grave-stones and crosses dating from the 5th century onwards.

There is a story that the two saints from opposite corners of the island used to meet at weekly intervals at a spot near Llannerch-y-medd, in the central north part of Anglesey. Cybi walking eastward in the morning and westward later in the day always had his face to the sun, and hence grew tanned; whereas Seiriol had the sun behind him on both trips, and remained pale. As a result, it is said, they were known as Cybi the Dark and Seiriol the Fair.

Throughout this period Puffin Island suffered with other spots in Anglesey from Viking raids. The Vikings had by the 9th century formed major centres at Dublin and in the Isle of Man, respectively 65 and 50 miles away. There were major invasions in 853, 877 and 902. The monasteries at Holyhead and Penmon were attacked in 961 and 971, and in 968 the royal palace at Aberffraw was destroyed.

The Vikings do not appear to have formed any sort of settlement, but their continuing presence is revealed in the survival of Norse names, not just those of the island itself and its offshoot Priestholm, but also of Osmund's. Eyre

*Penmon Priory*

*Capel Lligwy*

# THE COMING OF CHRISTIANITY

(now known as Gallows Point) near Beaumaris, and the rocky islets known as the Skerries which lie off Anglesey's north-west corner.

The end, or reduction, of Viking activity which seems to have taken place in the early 12th century, led to the realisation of Anglesey's potential prosperity. It was then that increased stability and the comparatively large population gave rise to the building of a large number of stone churches. The now ruined church of Capel Lligwy (14), a simple roofless structure in a field, is of this period, as is the older part of the double-aisled church of St Beuno at Aberffraw, where a very fine Norman arch of the period of Owain Gwynedd, the late 12th century, now decorates the west wall.

Also dedicated to Beuno, another lesser known of Anglesey's founding 'saints', is the church at Trefdraeth, south-west of Llangefni, though this dates from the next century, the 13th. One of Anglesey's most notable churches, by reason of its present position literally isolated on its rocky headland by the process of coastal erosion, is the 12th century foundation of St Cwyfan, 'the church in the sea' (15). Its primitive bare interior picks up the bleakness and austerity of its sea-surrounded position, and it is now seldom used.

Another fascinating church, though later and now ruined, is that on Llanddwyn Island off the sandy coast of Newborough Warren, between the south-west outflow of the Menai Strait and Malltraeth Bay. St Dwynwen is said to have built an oratory on the headland as early as the 5th century, after suffering an unhappy love affair. In Welsh tradition she became the patron saint of lovers, who used to make their pilgrimage to her well on Llanddwyn Island to seek to know from it whether their partner was faithful. Offerings were left at her shrine, and the monastery which administered this service became during Tudor times the richest church in the diocese of Bangor. The popularity of this cult led to the construction of a sizable church, in the early 16th century, the ruins of which now add a romantic feature to the atmosphere of this remote and now little visited piece of shore.

It is perhaps to this evidently settled period of the 12th century that Anglesey owes its reputation as the granary of Wales. The eventual achievement of the clearing of the forests had by then released the highly-fertile land of the boulder clay to cultivation, so that by the 12th century and increasingly in the 13th, Anglesey began to earn its now familiar title.

'Môn, Mam Cymru' is an old traditional saying: Anglesey, Mother of Wales — mother, in the sense of being the nation's supplier of food. It was said that just as the hills of Snowdonia could provide grazing for enough cattle to provide meat for the whole country, so the flat fertile fields of Anglesey could

*St Cwyfan's, 'the church in the sea'*

*The coffin of Princess Joan, at Beaumaris church*

# THE COMING OF CHRISTIANITY

supply enough grain. Giraldus wrote:

> The island of Mona is an arid and stony land, rough and unpleasant in
> its appearance, similar in its exterior qualities to the land of Pebidion,
> near St David's, but very different as to its interior value. For this
> island is incomparably more fertile in corn than any other part of
> Wales, from whence arose the British proverb, "Mon, mam Cymry,
> Mona, mother of Wales"; and when the crops have been defective in
> all other parts of the country, this island, from the richness of its soil
> and abundant produce, has been able to supply all Wales.

Llywelyn the Great, whose involvement with Anglesey we shall be
discussing in the next chapter, built himself many courts and manors
throughout his territory of North Wales, and frequently founded Christian
centres near to these. One such was at Llanfaes, not far from the ancient
monastic settlement of Penmon and the later fortified town of Beaumaris.
There he established a manor, and from the year 1237 installed a group of
Franciscan monks. His wife Joan, the daughter of King John of England, died
in that year, and the monastery formed her burial place. There is nothing to be
seen of this considerable site at ground level, but field names and the name of a
house, The Friars, or Fryars House, indicated its whereabouts, and in 1991 the
Gwynedd Archeological Trust undertook some trial excavations which
revealed structures and burials almost certainly associated with the Franciscan
friary. Further work was done in 1993, which produced a large amount of
medieval pottery.

# COURTS AND CASTLES

HEN Gildas, the contemporary source for 'dark age' history in Britain, refers to Maelgwn, King of Gwynedd, as 'draco insularis', 'the dragon of the island', he almost certainly identifies him as being closely associated with Anglesey. The kings of Gwynedd, like the later princes, had royal courts at various key points of their kingdoms, since no doubt it was necessary for them to be seen to be physically present and in command on a periodic basis wherever they reigned — a requirement which in due course led to the almost constant 'progress' made by medieval monarchs.

Because of this close connection of the king with the island it is highly likely that the royal court at Aberffraw, which we know was attacked by Vikings in 968, had become established by the time of Maelgwn, the mid-6th century. Since we know that it flourished in the days of Llywelyn the Great, who was known by the title of 'Prince of Aberffraw and Lord of Snowdon', it must have been in existence for some seven hundred years, and not (as the castles of equivalent age are now) as a ruin, but as a living feature.

In view of this great fame and continuity, of its status of unrivalled importance during this significant period of our history, it is particularly remarkable that there is nothing to be seen at Aberffraw of the thing that made it famous. More than the usual effort of imagination is needed to associate the quiet riverside village, with its fine double-aisled church and its two substantial chapels, little more now than a cluster of modest cottages on one small street, with a centre of administration of kings and princes governing North Wales. (17)

The site of the palace is now a field, distinguished only by a long low bank near the brow of its gentle slope (18), from which however there is a view down over the tidal inlet and out across Caernarfon Bay which explains much. It is a place with a good sea access, and once one stands there, outside the village, it then takes only a little more imagination to see the fleet of the Irish king arriving to take home the princess Branwen as his bride.

The reason, of course, that nothing now remains of the palace at Aberffraw is that throughout its long history it was made of wood. There are very few stone structures left of the period of the independent princes — Dolwyddelan Castle and Llywelyn's Tower at Conwy stand out — simply because very few were built. Churches were being built in stone from the time of the Norman conquest of England onwards, but the Norman custom of constructing

*'The Princes', a sculpture by Jonah Jones at Aberffraw*

*Site of the palace of the princes, at Aberffraw*

stone-built castles spread more slowly into Wales, and domestic buildings continued to be customarily made of wood. Wood, we must remember, was still plentiful; and in fact the use of it in building must have contributed to the clearance of the forests and the consequent opening up of fertile land.

The palace at Aberffraw actually remained in existence after its use had ended, with the Plantagenet invasion of North Wales and the loss of independence of the princes. It was not demolished until 1317, in fact, when its timbers were taken down to be used in the repair and improvement of Caernarfon Castle, during the last period of its construction which left it in its present form.

Documentary evidence also pointed to a court of Llywelyn's at the village of Rhosyr, which later (as we shall see) became Newborough. Llywelyn issued a charter from there in 1237. In 1992-3 the Gwynedd Archeological Trust excavated a field promisingly called Cae Llys (field of the court), which lies near St Peter's church on the hill outside the village. It is an unremarkable spot, but the highest ground around and within sight of the sea at Caernarfon Bay. There they found, sure enough, the substantial bases of walls, buried under several feet of sand, and pottery dating from the 13th and 14th centuries. Further excavation in 1994 found extensive stone foundations and signs of a large building, perhaps a hall. Excavation continued in 1995, when the expansive outside wall of the court was found, and another building within it.

# COURTS AND CASTLES

The stone walls of these structures, standing to a few feet high, are eloquently sturdy, and the whole complex covers a surprisingly large area. Coins again date the use of the site to a period from the mid 13th century. That we have here a rare identification of the precise site of one of Llywelyn's courts seems almost certain, and further work may yet produce more details of it.

The Kingdom of Gwynedd, during the early Middle Ages, consisted of more than the present county, incorporating most of Clwyd and Powys and at times having power over larger areas of mid and even southern Wales. Rhodri Mawr, who ruled from his seat at Aberffraw from 844-878 A.D., probably came as near as any member of this dynasty to being the overlord of all of Wales. He had inherited the succession derived from Maelgwn (on the dying out of the direct male line) from his grandmother, and the kingdom of Powys also fell to him on the death of his uncle, and as he had married into the royal house of Ceredigion part of South Wales too on the death of his brother-in-law, the last king.

Rhodri in effect founded two royal lines, that through Gruffydd ap Cynan leading to Llywelyn the Great, and the succession through his grandson Hywel Dda leading in due course to the house of Tudor, which we shall be encountering again.

The process by which the tension between the independent princedom ruled by Llywelyn the Great and the English monarchy grew until it led to the open conflict which destroyed that independence under his grandson Llywelyn the Last is a matter for Wales as a whole, rather than specifically Anglesey. In North Wales the hostility had always been not so much with the English king as with his representative, the Earl of Chester. And in the year 1090 the Normans arrived in Anglesey, under the leadership of Hugh of Avranches, Earl of Chester.

At this early date they built the motte style of castle prevalent at the time, at a site near a stream not far from the coast at Penmon, known as Aber Lleiniog. There, in a wood now reached by a small unmarked path, stands Hugh's fine mound, topped by the low but sturdy ruins of a stone-built castle. Hugh's original, however, was undoubtedly made of wood, and this present structure is a later medieval one.

The Welsh under the leadership of Gruffydd ap Cynan, the descendant of the royal house of Gwynedd, captured the original Norman castle in 1094, a setback to the invasion which caused the Normans to abandon their designs on Anglesey and indeed inner Gwynedd as a whole for the next hundred years.

Throughout this period Anglesey's ambivalent ties with Ireland continued, and when one branch of the inheritance of Rhodri Mawr, represented by

19

*Beaumaris castle's outer wall and moat*

# COURTS AND CASTLES

Gruffydd ap Llywelyn, took control of Gwynedd in 1039 from the rightful heir, the latter fled to Dublin (at that time of course a Viking city) and there took a Norse wife, and his son returned in due course to Anglesey with an army of rather unruly Viking mercenaries. This son, Gruffydd ap Cynan, who was to be the next Prince, was therefore half Viking, and it was almost certainly due to his friendship with the Norsemen of Dublin and the Isle of Man that Anglesey was relieved of the pressures of war, and enabled to embark on its period of church-building and agricultural expansion, in the first decades of the 12th century, which we noted in the last chapter.

When Gruffydd ap Cynan died, in 1137, at the then remarkable age of 82, his son Owain Gwynedd was able to succeed him in a kingdom secure, stable and prosperous, and it is to his reign, the second half of the 12th century, that such fine works as the Norman arch at Aberffraw and the original priory church at Penmon belong. Ironically it was the defeat of their former enemies, the Norsemen, which endangered the Princes of Aberffraw and eventually ended this period of peace. In 1170 the Norman kings of England took the Viking city of Dublin, and thus controlled both the land and the sea surrounding Gwynedd.

When the conflict between the English king and the Princes of Aberffraw reached its culmination in the war of 1276-7, the declining fortune of Llywelyn ap Gruffydd, Llywelyn the Last, was partly due to the recognition by Edward I of the importance of Anglesey to Welsh survival. Just as the island could supply the whole country with grain, so the country could not endure the loss of that supply. Edward therefore sent a fleet to blockade the corn supply, in fact seizing the harvest for his own use, echoing (no doubt unconsciously) Tacitus' observation that Anglesey was 'feeding the native resistance'.

In the final war of 1282 Edward employed precisely the same tactics. He sent an army from Rhuddlan to Anglesey in August, in order to commandeer the harvest. Once Anglesey was taken a bridge of boats was built across the Menai Strait, with the aim of launching a two-sided attack on Snowdonia. Through an inexplicable lack of co-ordination the English force was caught on the bridge and routed by the Welsh in November, 1282, and only the unforseen death of Llywelyn in December saved the situation for Edward. The bridge of boats remained, remarkably, in use for several months, being removed when the start of the construction of Caernarfon Castle required a free passage through the Strait.

Edward did indeed display his roots as a tactician by duplicating many of the steps of the Roman invasion of North Wales, more than a thousand years later.

19

*Beaumaris Castle from the air*

*The gateway to the castle*

34

# COURTS AND CASTLES

He was supplied, like them, by sea from Chester. He secured his advance, like them, by two crucial fortresses, one on the river at Conwy, and the other at Caernarfon. Like the Romans he did not seek an immediate stronghold on the island of Anglesey itself.

Caernarfon Castle was built in the mid 1280's, but the work was uncompleted when it suffered a severe setback when it was taken by the Welsh rebels led by Madog, Llywelyn's heir, in the major rising of the early 1290's. It is significant that the building of Beaumaris Castle began after this rebellion had been put down, making it by far the latest of Edward's Welsh castles.

A sizable town had already come into being nearby at Llanfaes, where a port and ferry-service operated in conjunction with Llywelyn's court and the monastery which he founded. It was noted as a place of some importance in 1254, when boats from Llanfaes were trading in Liverpool, and it was clearly by then a major port and commercial centre, becoming also the centre of Anglesey's important fishing industry. The ferry from Llanfaes, a significant feature during the Middle Ages, ran not to the mainland shoreline but to the edge of Lafan sands, at low tide, to which travellers would come on foot along a track across the sands.

Madog's rebellion of 1294 was rashly supported by the people of Llanfaes, and the town suffered the immediate wrath of Edward I, who was in the area. He not only destroyed the manor and the town, but deprived its people of the privileges they had derived from the independent princes, which he had previously confirmed. Edward arrived in Llanfaes in April, 1295, and stayed there for some weeks arranging the construction of a castle and garrison town.

Edward did not this time choose the same site for building his new fortress, but planned it on a stretch of level ground which had previously been a marsh. It is from this feature, it seems, that the town of Beaumaris gets its rather unexpected name: Beau Marais, fine marsh.

The rise of Beaumaris due to the king's decision led at once to the final decline of Llanfaes, and in fact the inhabitants of that area were (much against their will) moved out of the way of the military instrument to a village in south-western Anglesey previously known as Rhosyr, which hence became known as Newborough, in 1303. All the town's trade had in any case been transferred to Beaumaris, by way of its port rights, its weekly market and annual fairs; even the houses themselves were moved to Beaumaris, and the once prosperous and important borough of Llanfaes was effectively wiped out of existence, leaving in the present scattered hamlet something of a challenge to our imagination.

The building of the castle which started in 1295 was not so much completed

# COURTS AND CASTLES

as abandoned in 1298, since it was never actually finished. This fact perhaps coincides with the point that it was never actually used either, as a military weapon, and one wonders whether it became apparent that the decision to defend this end of the Strait as well as the Caernarfon end was not quite as astute as Edward's planning usually was. Its existence did of course mean that Beaumaris became the administrative and legal centre of the island, and this was no doubt part of its original purpose. The castle was much used as a prison throughout its active life, and it was chiefly this function which maintained its garrison.

Because of its late date and because its site was not obstructed by previous buildings or by any natural features, Beaumaris castle represents a perfect model of the theoretical concentric form of defensive structure (19). A moat surrounds an outer wall which surrounds a stronger rectangle around an inner ward. Inside, it is surprisingly spacious, its firm symmetry giving a feeling of soundness and security. This, however, is about all the effect it produces, since its low-lying position and the lack of views towards it give it a rather tame, domestic aspect, quite unlike the awesome military seriousness of Conwy or the decorative regality of Caernarfon.

The inner structure in particular remains impressive and well-preserved, in spite of this lack of immediate impact. One notes the sophistication of the defensive form: the outer gates set at an angle to the larger inner ones, preventing a direct assault; the projecting towers on all the walls, providing cover to their outer bases. Unfinished was a North Gate in the curtain wall, and the walls of the town itself, which have now almost entirely disappeared, were added as something of an afterthought a hundred years later. The town is thus, again unlike Conwy and Caernarfon, something of a separate unit.

The castle played a brief role in the Civil War, when the leading Anglesey family, the Bulkeleys, held it for the king before surrendering it to General Mytton and the Parliamentary army in 1646.

Once formed, the town of Beaumaris went from strength to strength, and we shall be reviewing some of its development in the next chapter.

20

# THE TUDORS,
# AND OTHER FAMILIES

DOWN an obscure narrow lane some two miles west of Llangefni lies a sturdy stonebuilt house. Though recently restored, it is still something of a hotchpotch of fashions and periods, and only the style of the chimneys and main doorway conveys an air of age and authority.

This is Plas Penmynydd (21), notable for being the family home of the original Tudor family, whose name, by a series of accidents, grew from its roots here in Anglesey to become almost synonymous with Britain's rise to universal influence at the time of the Renaissance.

Plas Penmynydd was built in 1576, presumably on the site of a medieval forebear, and largely rebuilt in the 17th century, with additions in the 19th. It bears, however, the Tudor arms on its exterior, and the same reappear in the little church nearby, a building mainly of the period of the turn of the 14th to the 15th centuries. There lie the effigies of Gronw Fychan (20) and his wife, who died in about 1385, finely carved figures in alabaster on a substantial altar-tomb, which bears some shields showing the Tudor arms, also present on the surcoat of the knight — for these were the ancestors of that family.

The name Tudor first appears in Anglesey as a Christian name, being that of one of the sons of Ednyfed Fychan, the right-hand man of Llywelyn the Great, whose family received extensive lands and privileges as a reward for his loyal and distinguished support for the Prince. It is equivalent to the European name Theodore, and some members of the lineage later called themselves by the version. In its Welsh form it should correctly be pronounced 'Tidder', and interestingly it was evidently thus pronounced at the time when the future Henry VII was posing a threat to the reining monarch. Richard III. In the fateful July of 1485 the latter issued from Westminster a proclamation, which includes the words:

> The said Traitors have chosen to be their Captain one Henry Tydder, son of Edmund Tydder, whom of his ambitions and insatiable covetise encroacheth and usurpeth upon him, the name and title of Royal Estate of this realm of England . . .

Less than a month later came the Battle of Bosworth and the radical change to the monarchy of England which had such far-reaching consequences. How did all this issue from Penmynydd?

*Tomb of Gronw Fychan, ancestor of the Tudors*

*Plas Penmynydd, family seat of the Tudors*

*Beaumaris Church*

# THE TUDORS, AND OTHER FAMILIES

Ironically the Tudor family of Penmynydd had reached the peak of their influence and prominence in the 14th century, and by the time their name became famous they were, at home, in decline. The Tudors, along with other great lines descended from Ednyfed Fychan, had risen to figure as major landowners in Anglesey before and immediately after Edward I's conquest of North Wales, in the 1280's, when family lands were largely successfully retained by Ednyfed's leading descendants. They rose to further prominence by supporting (to begin with) the English throne. Two brothers, Rhys and Gwilym, were with Richard II during his last tragic years, and probably even witnessed his deposition by Bolingbroke during his fatal journey through North Wales.

This allegiance no doubt coloured their attitude to the rebellion which broke out in North Wales shortly after, itself stirred by dissatisfaction with the new usurping king. But in any case its leader, Owain Glyndŵr, was their first cousin, and it was in the ensuing fiasco that the Tudor family lost their natural caution, and with it their status and fortune. In the case of Rhys and Gwilym ap Tudor it seems that they also literally lost their heads, since on the collapse of Glyndŵr's revolt Rhys, at least, seems to have been executed at Chester. The most notable exploit of the brothers during the rebellion was the taking, for Glyndŵr, of Conwy Castle, which they stormed with their Anglesey followers in April 1401.

The outcome of this choice of the wrong side was the temporary loss to the family of Penmynydd itself, which they did not regain until 1430. From then on the estate, which had formerly been considerable, continued to dwindle through the continuing of the custom of inheritance by subdivision, which persisted in Anglesey into the 16th century. It is thus that the irony arose that as the family rose to fame elsewhere its root stock, once so powerful, declined in importance to the status of country squires.

Meanwhile the nephew of the brothers we have referred to, Owain Tudor, had left Anglesey to better himself elsewhere. He became an attendant at the court of Henry V, went with the army to France, and probably even fought, along with other Welshmen, at the Battle of Agincourt. After Henry's death he gained the post of clerk of the wardrobe in the Queen's household, at the time when the heir, Henry VI, was still an infant, and the Queen-mother herself in fact only 21 years old.

Catherine de Valois, widow of Henry V, was the daughter of King Charles VI of France. We do not quite know how, but the Welshman gained her favour, and amazingly in 1429 they seem to have undertaken a secret marriage. It was thus that Henry VI's half-brothers were Tudors, and through them, and

*Effigies on a Bulkeley tomb in Beaumaris Church*

*Drawing of Henblas, the original home of the Bulkeleys*

# THE TUDORS, AND OTHER FAMILIES

the marriage of Edmund Tudor into the Lancastrian line, Henry VII in due course derived a somewhat dubious claim to the throne.

The rest is history, and unfortunately would take us too far from Anglesey to be recited here. Owain Tudor, though for a time in trouble, was pardoned by the king and sent home to Anglesey in 1439, and as a supporter of the Lancastrian cause he was imprisoned and beheaded after the Yorkists' victory at Mortimer's Cross in 1461.

While the Tudor family in Anglesey was declining in importance during the 15th century, at the same time the family which was to become Anglesey's leading one thereafter was coming into prominence. From then until now the name Bulkeley has been associated with the island as a whole, and particularly with the town and area of Beaumaris, where they made their seat.

In many cases in Wales the rise of the landed gentry took place during the period of the Tudor monarchy in England, when the Act of Union gave to Welshmen the same opportunities to succeed through the holding of high office both in Wales and at the English court, as that held by their English counterparts. In such cases it was often previous office-holders who rose, but the Bulkeleys were new to Anglesey and seem to have started their rise to power simply through the acquisition of property.

William Bulkeley moved from Cheadle in Cheshire to Beaumaris in about 1444. The reasons for his move are not clear, but he seems to have been already a wealthy man. He then married into a local landowning family, (one which, like the Tudors, owed their estates to their descent from Ednyfed Fychan), quickly rose to personal position and together with his wife to the ownership of substantial property in Beaumaris. He and his wife set about acquiring lands in other parts of Anglesey, and when their son married into a family of the Conwy valley area the Bulkeleys came to own extensive lands there as well. Although their influence thus became widespread, they retained in particular their close connection with Beaumaris.

When he died in 1490 William Bulkeley left £20 in his will for a tomb for him and his wife. It is very probably this tomb which we may see now in Beaumaris church, a fine pair of alabaster figures on an altar-tomb. (22) There is some evidence, however, to suggest that the figures are rather Rowland Bulkeley, their son, who died in 1537, and his wife Alice; but as the dress is late 15th century this seems less likely.

The parish church of St Mary and St Nicholas is itself full of reminders of the Bulkeley family, though in fact it originated before their time, being largely of early 14th century date. It has a large and airy interior and a fine sturdy exterior, all of which gives a more impressive effect than one would expect in a

*Timber framed house in Castle Street, Beaumaris*

*Victoria Terrace, Beaumaris*

*Beaumaris gaol*

small country town. It is strikingly well preserved and maintained, and continues to testify to the importance and prosperity of Beaumaris.

Beaumaris church's main claim to fame has already been mentioned: the preservation here, in its church porch, of the stone coffin of Princess Joan, wife of Llywelyn the Great. The plaque which accompanies it is worth recording:

> This plain *Sarcophagus* (once dignified, as having contained the remains of *JOAN* daughter of King *JOHN*, and consort of *LLEWELYN* ap *IORWERTH* Prince of *North Wales*, who died in the year 1237) having been conveyed from the Friary of *Llanfaes*, and, alas! used for many years as a horse-watering trough, was rescued from such indignity, and placed here for preservation, as well as to excite serious meditations on the transitory nature of all sublunary distinctions. By THOMAS JAMES WARREN BULKELY, *Viscount* BULKELEY. Oct. 1808.

One feature which the town unfortunately lacks is the Bulkeleys' original home, Henblas, which must have been one of the finest houses on Anglesey. It was built in the late 15th century by William Bulkeley, on a site on the corner of Church Street and Margaret Street, with what became the market forming its yard, and its gardens extending to the town wall. The whole complex evidently occupied a large area, and from drawings made before it was demolished it can be seen to have been in the styles of several successive periods.(23) It was sadly demolished in 1869.

By then it was no longer the family's principal seat, but had become a dower property when the Bulkeleys moved, in the early 17th century, to Baron Hill, built by Sir Richard Bulkeley, a man of great standing and popularity at the courts of Elizabeth I and James I.

Baron Hill now is itself a ruin, since the family have moved again to another of their properties nearby. So closely surrounded by trees that it can hardly be seen, it is now elusive and obscure. The original had in any case not survived, since the whole thing was reconstructed in the last century. The tall column nearby, known as the Bulkeley Memorial, dates from the late 19th century, when it was erected in memory of one of the more prominent and popular of the Bulkeley baronets, one of many Sir Richards.

The town of Beaumaris itself, now displaying an air of prosperity and solidity more common in mid-Wales and the borders than on this coast, has always to some extent been an English settlement, although to begin with its population included a surprisingly strong Welsh element, including a number of prosperous and influential individuals evidently persisting there from the

*Plas Newydd, home of the Marquess of Anglesey*

# THE TUDORS, AND OTHER FAMILIES

days of Llanfaes.

Like the other towns built by Edward I it was laid out in the simple grid pattern of a medieval borough, Church Street and Castle Street forming then, as they form now, its main axes. The sea originally came up to the castle and to the town's frontage, and it was as a port, mainly, that Beaumaris rose to prosperity.

There are no buildings of its original period left intact, although the timber-framed house in Castle Street, parts of the back of which date from about 1400, gives an impression of what the town must once have looked like. (24) It was much altered in the 17th century, when its frontage took the form it now has. Much of the substantial air of the town originates from its early coaching days, and it is to the 17th century that such fine old inns as the George and Dragon, the Bull's Head and the Liverpool Arms belong. The court house, which ones passes en route to the castle, is also of this period, being built in 1614.

The most striking feature of Beaumaris is perhaps the sea frontage, in the form of the Bulkeley Arms hotel and, especially, Victoria Terrace, a block built in a grand classical style in the 1830's, testament to Beaumaris's increasing connection with quarrying and the trade in limestone (25). One other stone-built and notable building is the town's gaol, which lies behind the church, now closely surrounded by streets and buildings (26). Built in 1829, it remains virtually unaltered, and therefore provides an interesting record of its time. Its interior now gives an insight into the Victorian penal system, the cells, the location of the scaffold, even the treadmill still in place.

During much of the period in which the Bulkeley estate at Baron Hill has dominated this side of the island, the Plas Newydd estate, seat of the Marquesses of Anglesey, has formed its most prominent neighbour to the south.

Like so many great houses, the present Plas Newydd (27) is the descendant of a succession of previous structures, starting in the late 15th and early 16th centuries. The present graceful building dates largely from alterations made between 1783 and 1785, together with improvements to the interior, including the elegant staircase, and to the west facade, made by James Wyatt and Joseph Potter in 1795. The intentionally Gothic appearance which they then imposed on the outside of the building has been modified to its current more welcoming character by the removal of the battlements which ran round the parapet, by the 6th Marquess in the 1930's.

The family, originally part of the distinguished local Griffith family of Penrhyn, had achieved even greater substance by marriage into the Paget

28

*The Marquess of Anglesey's column*

# THE TUDORS, AND OTHER FAMILIES

family of Staffordshire, in 1737, from which they inherited a barony, the name being changed to Paget in the process. The Pagets themselves were descended from a prominent adviser to Henry VIII, and had in the interim produced a succession of courtiers and diplomats. By the time of the marriage of the Griffith heir, Sir Nicholas Bayly, to Caroline Paget, they had accumulated considerable property in the Midlands, some areas of which were to prove fruitful sources of coal. In 1784 Lord Paget was created Earl of Uxbridge, and this remained the family's chief title until 1815.

Lord Uxbridge established himself, in competition with other local magnates, as the most prominent person in Anglesey and the Caernarfon area, and expanded the family fortunes by opening up the exploitation of the rich copper seams of Parys Mountain, which we shall be investigating in the next chapter. When he died in 1812 his eldest son had already begun his highly distinguished military career, and subsequently occupied the honourable position of second-in-command to the Duke of Wellington at the Battle of Waterloo. On that battlefield he lost a leg, and in recognition of his services to the victory he was created Marquess of Anglesey, on 4th July, 1815.

The column commemorating this hero, which stands above the road approaching Llanfairpwll, was erected in 1816, although the statue of the Marquess was not added until 1860 (28). Its 115 steps are climbed by over 5,000 visitors a year, who gain from its top a magnificent view over Anglesey in one direction and towards the mountains of Snowdonia in the other. The one-legged veteran himself, like his colleague the Duke, pursued a varied political life after the war, and remained active in public service well into his 80's.

Plas Newydd, much of its Strait-side woodland, and its garden, the latter originally designed by Humphry Repton at the turn of the 18th and 19th centuries, were given to the National Trust in 1976, and are now visited by some 53,000 people each year. The house still remains nevertheless very much the home of the present Marquess, who occupies a top-floor flat. It houses a remarkable mural by Rex Whistler, painted for the 6th Marquess between 1937 and 1940 as decoration for a new dining room, and two military museums one of which is largely devoted to the subject of Waterloo.

On the lawns above Plas Newydd, past which the visitor approaches, is a well-preserved cromlech, a neolithic burial chamber. From that perspective through the mineral wealth of the 18th century, to the blossoming of architecture, landscape and art of the 19th and 20th, indeed to its role in the island's welfare at the present day, Plas Newydd offers us something of a potted history of some aspects of Anglesey's development.

# THE TUDORS, AND OTHER FAMILIES

In particular we are reminded of the island's habit of keeping contact with a wider world. These features of Plas Newydd, from the stone-age cromlech to the Whistler mural, are examples of the high style of their times. Even the fact that it could influence, and be influenced by, an event so remote from it as the Battle of Waterloo, is an instance of how Anglesey has, for an island, remained in many ways remarkably uninsular.

29

# SOURCES OF WEALTH

NGLESEY'S ability to influence and be influenced by outside events is demonstrated again in the story of its sources of wealth. What, one might well wonder, has the history of gun-making to do with Amlwch?

During the 14th century cannons had come to be made largely of iron, at first cast and later wrought, and it was not until about 1520 that the emphasis changed significantly to making guns out of bronze. More specifically a variety of bronze known as gun-metal was used, this being particularly resistant to corrosion. Although gun-metal as understood now is an alloy of which 88% consists of copper, in its earlier form the copper content was 90%. Two other factors combined to produce, from this fact, a sharp rise in the value of copper.

The increase in importance of ordnance in warfare was an inevitable outcome of the trend to improved technology. This coincided with an independence of national attitude fostered by the Tudor monarchy, which led to policies of resistance to imports and hence to the tendency to open up home resources. Imported ores were in any case expensive, and became more so as a result of taxation. Imported cannons were likewise an undesirable burden on the defence budget.

Consequently the copper-mining industry, which had previously been largely a royal monopoly, was opened up to private competition by the late 17th century. Adding to the military uses an increasing use of the metal in coins and household items, we have the circumstances for a copper boom set to erupt at the beginning of the 18th century.

Finds of hammer stones on Parys Mountain, near Amlwch, indicate that copper may have been mined there in prehistoric times, and crushing stones of a possibly Roman period have also been found. Continuing work promises to reveal a rich prehistoric past. The 18th century traveller, Thomas Pennant, reported remains of ancient trenches and pieces of charcoal, signs of early quarrying, since in pre-gunpowder days the ore would be extracted by cracking the rock through heating it and cooling it suddenly with water. Pennant attributes these operations to the Romans, "as the Britons imported all works in brass".

Although there had been no exploitation of Anglesey's copper between the Roman period and the 17th century (when its existence is referred to) it was evidently known of all along, but regarded until the boom came as of little

*Ruins on Parys Mountain*

53

*Old print of the copper workings on Parys Mountain*

*Parys Mountain today*

value. Indeed the copper's medicinal qualities seem to have been more highly regarded than its financial one.

Parys Mountain is one of Anglesey's rare eminences, its modest 480 feet of altitude rising above the northern part of the island with conspicious dominance. What is remarkable about it is that it seems to have been largely composed of copper; and also that as a result the whole of the inside of the mountain has been taken away (29).

The result of this in that the inside of Parys Mountain now presents a quite remarkable sight, somewhere between a miniature version of the Grand Canyon and the interior of a volcano's crater. Its geology is made visible by the cross-section effect of the quarrying. The layered strata of its makeup twist and buckle, clearly showing the pressures of internal forces. Its varied mineral content gives its rock-faces quite unrock-like colours, black, red, green. Altogether it is now an unearthly place.

Robert Parys was a 15th century government official, who was given this lump of land, formerly known as Mynydd Trysglwyn, as a reward for collecting fines, on behalf of Henry IV, from supporters of Glyndŵr's failed rebellion. It had fallen into a mixture of ownership before the copper discovery, in which the influence of Sir Nicholas Bayly was dominant. Sir Nicholas, as mentioned in the previous chapter, was the grandfather of the first Marquess of Anglesey.

The copper mining here developed at a comparatively late date, and rose spectacularly to a remarkable peak before declining equally suddenly. It was in progress by the 1760's and lasted from then for some sixty to seventy years.

The further rise in demand which sparked it off was supplied by requirements of naval warfare, in which it became the fashion to coat the ships' hulls with a plating of copper below the waterline. Later the bolts which secured this were also made of copper. In response to this increased demand, Bayly introduced a mining firm into Anglesey in 1764. For a time little activity took place, until an exceptionally rich seam was discovered in 1768.

Bayly's neighbours on the mountain started mining in the 1770's, and the Parys Mine Company was formed in 1778, by Bayly's neighbour and partly co-owner of the mountain's properties, the Rev. Edward Hughes, together with the latter's lawyer, Thomas Williams, who went on to become a person of great standing in Britain as a whole at the rise of the industrial age. It was this Anglesey entrepreneur, the son of a local farmer, who eventually built up, and controlled, the British copper industry, achieving a monopoly also of the Cornish mines in the late 1780's.

Bayly leased his share of the land mined by the Parys Mine Company for 21

*Porth Amlwch*

# SOURCES OF WEALTH

years, and his son, Henry Paget, who became first Earl of Uxbridge, formed the Mona Mine Company in 1785 on the remainder of his land there. The enterprising Thomas Williams was a partner in that firm as well, with a quarter share.

Pennant, meanwhile, visited Anglesey in 1778, and his description of the mines in operation is impressive. It was, he said, "the most considerable body of copper ore perhaps ever known". The mighty workings of extraction and purification seem to have caused horrendous polution:

> Suffocating fumes issue from the burning heaps of copper, and extend their baneful influence for miles around. In the adjacent parts vegetation is nearly destroyed; even the mosses and lichens of the rocks have perished . . .

Pennant estimates that the 1,500 people employed accounted, with their families, for some 8,000 of the population of Anglesey, dependant on the mines. Workers had been attracted from other parts of Wales and later from Cornwall, leaving, apparently, a remnant of families of distant Cornish origin still to be found in the Amlwch area. In addition to the work of extraction a smelting industry developed at Amlwch, which could take ore from elsewhere, and inevitably Amlwch became, by stages, a port, and expanded from the former small village into a prosperous market town (30).

During the late 18th century the workers were paid by the Parys Mine Company in copper tokens, its own minted penny and halfpenny coins, literally worth their weight in copper, their value consequently rising and falling with the market. The coins, which became collector's pieces at an early date, bear a druid's head on the observe, and on the reverse the letters PMC and the date.

At their peak the mines are estimated to have produced a yield of 44,000 tons of ore per year. The ore was obtained by a combination of blasting and quarrying, and also by the use of ponds to gather the precipitation from the water flowing from the workings.

The companies seem to have faltered towards the end of the 18th century, but became reformed into a new combination, and work continued into the 19th century. But just as demand had risen with war, so the conclusion of the Napoleonic wars (to which the Marquess of Anglesey had, ironically, contributed) led to a critical decrease in the value of copper, so that from 1815 onwards the Anglesey mines became less viable. The quantity of ore still available, however, enabled production to remain high, even though its great rewards were now reduced. There were a number of recoveries before the final

*The restored windmill at Llanddeusant*

# SOURCES OF WEALTH

decline. A brief rise in price increased the prosperity of the Mona Mine Company in the 1820's but both this and a second respite in the 1830's were short-lived.

Further reversals of the same factors as had given rise to the initial success led to the venture's eventual cessation. The home industry was deprived of the protection awarded it by the Tudors in a new political climate which favoured free trade, when duties on imported ores were removed in the mid-19th century. The mines were gradually abandoned from then on, and though they struggled on in a small way until the end of the century they were no longer of any significance after the 1850's.

Although it must rank as its major source of wealth, copper mining was not the only industry common in Anglesey during those centuries. The extraction of limestone also developed into something of a major industry, as may be seen today along the coast from Penmon point. Originally quarried only for local use, its high quality eventually ensured for it an export market.

Farming continued, though the higher wages offered by the mines sometimes made this difficult to sustain, particularly in the Amlwch area. In particular the plentiful supply of corn which was Anglesey's hallmark gave rise to a flourishing milling industry, powered by both wind and water, the results of which can still be seen dotted around the island today.

There are unfortunately few remains now of the water mills, but the towers of the windmills have in many cases survived. Most of these date from the 18th and 19th centuries. The Royal Commission on Ancient Monuments reports that in 1929 37 windmills were recorded, some of them still possessing their sails. Now the sails have gone, and many of the towers are converted into dwellings. One, however, the Llynon Mill at Llanddeusant, has recently been restored by Anglesey Borough Council and is now the only working windmill in Wales (31). Having fallen out of use in the 1920's, after suffering damage in a storm in 1918, it was bought by the Council in 1978, and restoration using the original internal workings, but with the need for new woodwork, took place between then and its opening to the public in May, 1984. It now receives some 18,000 visitors a year, being open to the public from Easter to the end of September, Tuesdays to Saturdays, and bank holidays, 11.00 to 5.00, and Sundays 1.00 to 5.00. The ground floor is occupied by the Anglesey Craftworkers Guild, who provide an exhibition there during these times. Another mill in a state of near completion is the Kingsland Mill at Holyhead, although in this case the top was removed, after suffering damage, during the last war.

It was of course farming which supported the economy of the island for the

# SOURCES OF WEALTH

long period between the decline of the copper mines and the rise of modern industry, although its reputation for crop growing has been replaced to some extent by an acknowledgement of the quality of its grassland, and the thriving market at Llangefni testifies to Anglesey's ability to fatten cattle and sheep. This background sustenance, the heritage of the good soil formed by the boulder clay, continued and continues throughout is history; but inevitably an island has another nature also, that of its coastline, and Anglesey's character has always been to some extent maritime. It was the rise in the importance of travel and communications during the early part of the last century which threw an unexpected emphasis on this aspect of its nature, and brought about perhaps the most radical change to take place in the whole of the island's history.

# THE PORT OF IRELAND

I T was, wrote William Morris in 1759, "Common these days to see two or three postchaises arriving at Holyhead at the same time."

The traffic problem had started. Where, we may wonder, were these intrepid travellers going? The fact is that from the middle of the 18th century onwards the expansion of the cities and the increase of trade and social communication between them took place in combination.

Dublin, in particular, came into its own at this period, and its commerce with London increased dramatically in importance. At the same time the northern cities of Liverpool and Manchester underwent a radical change in size and importance, the prelude to their participation in the industrial revolution.

In addition to this new demand from commerce, the improving turnpike roads which resulted started to be used, at this time, by the first tourists. We have already seen how Thomas Pennant travelled through Wales, making three tours in the years between 1773 and 1776. In that same decade, in the summer of 1774, the great Dr Johnson travelled from Denbighshire through North Wales, during which adventure he informs Boswell that he "passed over into Anglesea". He was not, however, greatly impressed: "Wales is so little different from England, that it offers nothing to the speculation of the traveller." Besides these distinguished writers, whose records have survived to be still available, a host of lesser diarists and letter-writers record more obscurely their journeys here at this time, the mid and later 18th century.

There are records (as has been mentioned) of ferries operating at Llanfaes as early as the 13th century, and at Beaumaris from the early 14th, which indicates even at that time a degree of travel across Anglesey. We also know that there was a ferry at Porthaethwy, the area which became known as Menai Bridge, and nearby the 'bishop's ferry' ran from a spot below Upper Bangor known as Porthesgob to a point just east of Menai Bridge. Midway down the Strait another ferry is recorded at Llanidan, near Bryn Siencyn. Add to these a crossing at the western end of the Strait, at Abermenai, and we see that Anglesey was plentifully linked to the mainland through the Middle Ages and the 16th century.

There is no doubt from accounts which have survived from the 17th century that at least by then the main purpose of all this travel via Anglesey was to get to Ireland. The Holyhead Packet boats were in regular operation by then, and

*The Telford suspension bridge across the Menai Strait*

*Toll-houses designed by Thomas Telford.*
*Holyhead harbour*
*Inset: Archway commemorating the visit of George IV at the old harbour*

# THE PORT OF IRELAND

whatever efforts other towns in North Wales made to obtain the status of the port for Ireland, it seems as if Holyhead had already, before the issue arose, established itself as the natural bearer of this role. Indeed when Lord Clarendon made the journey in January 1696 he found no less than two yachts and three packets at Holyhead prepared to take him to Dublin. The reason for this apparent overprovision is the growing importance of the post, which must by then reach Dublin from London as speedily and regularly as possible.

It is not surprising that it should have been considered desirable to build a bridge across the Strait, to avoid the discomfort, danger, and more particularly the delays of the ferries; what is surprising is that it should have taken so long to achieve this. According to a story common locally in the 18th century Edward I himself had proposed to build a bridge at Bangor, but had been distracted from this task by other events. Whatever the truth of this there is no doubt that bridges were very much discussed both here and at Conwy from the turn of the 18th to the 19th century.

Towards the end of the 18th century various proposals were considered for crossing the narrows at the Swillies by embankment or by timber bridge, but navigational and tidal factors, together with local factional differences, overcame these schemes. Petitions to Parliament by the promoters however eventually led to the presentation of a Bill, in 1786, but even this failed to result in action. It was not until the engineer John Rennie arrived in the area in 1801, with instructions, presumably from Parliament, to study the problem of bridging the Menai, that the matter looked like becoming a reality.

As it happened the bridge for which Rennie produced a design never got built. His plan for cast-iron arches was grandiose and expensive, and times appear to have been hard. In 1810 the matter was considered again, and Rennie's scheme seems almost to have become adopted. It was the coincidence that Thomas Telford had also been appointed, by the Treasury, to survey the whole road system in North Wales, a commission which included recommending the best way of bridging the Menai Strait, which finally decided the issue.

Telford's original design was again a cast-iron arched bridge. We are perhaps fortunate that although the relevant committee approved this, there was some delay, during which time Telford was at work improving the North Wales roads. At this time he began to consider suspension by wrought-iron cables as an alternative to the traditional arched method of bridging, and a plan for such a bridge at Runcorn was produced in 1817. The next year he had submitted a design for a suspension bridge across the Menai, which was immediately approved.

*Britannia Bridge, Stephenson's railway bridge now adapted to take road traffic*

*The lifeboat station, Moelfre*

*South Stack lighthouse*

# THE PORT OF IRELAND

We thus have here the first, and probably the loveliest, major suspension bridge in Britain, indeed in the world. It was opened in January 1826, followed very soon after by the smaller version at Conwy. It was to be ten years before Brunel designed his Clifton Gorge bridge, which so much shows the Menai Bridge's influence, and a further hundred before the long-span giants of America took up Telford's initiative.

The famous bridge survives now in almost its original form, having been strengthened to take modern traffic by the replacement of its cables, between 1938 and 1941, when the former double carriageway was converted to a single one (32).

Thomas Telford was an architect as well as an engineer, and he personally designed every element of his schemes, down to the toll-gates themselves. An example of one of these gates, with their effect of crossing sun-rays, still remains in Anglesey, at the approach to the Penrhos nature reserve at the western end of the Stanley embankment, near Holyhead. One of Telford's toll-houses, which he also designed himself, is preserved there, and other examples of these, easily recognisable by their octagonal fronts, flank the A5 at Llanfairpwll, Gwalchmai and Caergeiliog (33). The road remained tolled until November, 1895, by which time it was the last remaining toll-road in Great Britain.

At the same time as Telford was building his crossing he constructed this new coach road, now the A5, to replace the narrow and winding one which had crossed Anglesey since the 16th century, bringing into being the equivalent of today's bypassing motorways. The old road still runs from village to village alongside it, and here and there one may spot a pre-Telford coaching inn, its business suddenly withdrawn in 1822. At the port of Holyhead steam, at this innovatory time, was replacing sail. Steam paddlers ran from 1817, and passengers crossed by a regular steam packet service from 1819. The Post Office started to operate its own steam service from there to Dublin in 1821, making the crossing in about half the time it had previously taken.

A Parliamentary sub-committee had in the meantime decided, as early as 1810, to build a proper harbour to take this increasing sea traffic. Sir John Rennie submitted a scheme for this, and although his plans for bridging the Menai had not been favoured against Telford's his is the credit for Holyhead's old harbour (34) and its buildings, dating from 1821. King George IV himself arrived at Holyhead on 7th August of that year, and crossed to Ireland on the paddling boat 'Lightning' (then renamed the 'Royal George IV') on August 12th.

# THE PORT OF IRELAND

This was indeed the age of progress, and the radical changes brought about by the new road system were followed within twenty years by one still more cataclysmic, the coming of the railway. The first train line had crossed Anglesey in 1848, but as yet there was no rail crossing of the Strait, and passengers must disembark and cross the water by road. Robert Stephenson had however been following quite closely Telford's example, though his bridges were cantilevered in tubular form, and the Menai tubular bridge (the 'Britannia Bridge') was opened in 1850, allowing a through train to run from London to Holyhead. Stephenson's original thin and elegant tube has unfortunately been considerably altered by the addition of arches, after being largely destroyed by fire in 1970, to strengthen it enough to support a road deck over the railway (35).

George Borrow, who preferred walking to riding in vehicles, noted with some disgust the arrival of the train to Holyhead, when he came this way in 1854: it passed, he writes in *Wild Wales*, "voiding fierce sparks, and making a terrible noise". He was obliged, noting the irony, to stay at the Railway Hotel, which must then have recently opened.

After the coming of the railway Holyhead harbour was further improved, in 1858, when the West Quay was opened. The inner harbour, with railway station and hotel, was not completed however until 1875, and was officially opened by the Prince of Wales in 1880, when the clock was erected to commemorate the event. Not much changed about the notably gloomy station from then on until recently, when the success of the 'seacat' ferries and the coming of a giant high-speed catamaran has brought Holyhead abruptly into the modern world. Now the terminal has been radically redesigned by the Manser (father and son) team of architects, the new highly modern architecture linking effectively to the original railway station.

In the meantime further, quite separate, works had taken place in the form of the construction of the breakwater. As early as 1828 Parliament had resolved to build, all over Britain, harbours of refuge, where passing ships could ride out a gale. This decision followed some remarkable and destructive storms of that year. Further emphasis was laid on this scheme, for the same reason, in 1839, although it was not until 1845 that work started on the Holyhead breakwater, under the direction of the civil engineer J.M. Rendell. It took in all 28 years to build, and was opened, also by the Prince of Wales, in 1873.

Although its function as a port for Ireland made it pre-eminent in Anglesey's maritime history, Holyhead was not the only sheltered harbour on the island. We have seen that Amlwch's harbour was improved in the 18th century to

# THE PORT OF IRELAND

cater for the copper trade, and in the 1820's and '30's it became something of a ship-building centre. Bull Bay, nearby, was to some extent its predecessor, being a landing-spot for ships from Liverpool before the development of Amlwch and later Holyhead. It also provided a pilot station and a lifeboat.

Lifeboats, and shipwrecks, in fact occupy a prominent place in the history of this northern and north-eastern coast, the turning point of the busy seaway out of Liverpool. Cemaes ran a lifeboat until the 1930's, and had in fact been a busy small port and ship-building area since at least the 18th century. A local diarist, William Bulkeley, provides us with a rare insight into the trading, and indeed smuggling, which took place there at that time.

Most notable and enduring of the many lifeboats around this coast is that of Moelfre, which still operates, responsible for the saving of literally hundreds of lives (36). It was founded in 1830, but its prowess was unequal to the notable gale of October, 1859, in which the clipper 'The Royal Charter' was wrecked in nearby Lligwy Bay.

'The Royal Charter', a steam-assisted sailing clipper, was homeward bound from Melbourne to her port of Liverpool. Her wreck carries the added romance of lost treasure, since although her cargo was sheepskins and wool her passengers, of whom there were 388, were mainly gold-diggers returning with their produce.

'The Royal Charter' went down in what was then the worst hurricane Britain had experienced in living memory, in which altogether 133 ships sank around the coasts of Britain. Of her 388 passengers and 112 ship's company 459 people lost their lives. Some of the gold was washed ashore shortly afterwards, some recovered subsequently, and some, probably, is still there. Certainly this wreck, out of the very many around this coast of Anglesey, continues to exert an influence on people's imaginations.

Anglesey's maritime character is brought out by its having its own Nelson monument, a stone statue of the great naval leader which stands on the foreshore of the Menai Strait just to the west of the railway crossing, a familiar sight to shipping passing through the Strait. It was erected by a member of the Paget family, himself an admiral, in 1873.

In keeping with the frequency of its passing shipping, Anglesey developed lighthouses at its northern end from an early period. That at Point Lynas now is the descendant of a house with two bright lights in its upstairs windows, which was constructed there in the 1780's. This was followed by the present building, constructed in 1835 by the Trustees of Liverpool Docks. The same body also instituted a chain of semaphore stations along the North Wales coast in the 1820's, the furthest from the port being that on Holyhead Mountain, and one at Point Lynas taking up the succession and passing it to a further tower on Puffin Island, from where the message crossed the bay to the Great Orme. In this way the merchants of Liverpool could gain advance warning of the arrival of their ships. The messages usually made the journey in as short a time as four minutes, and in a demonstration run in 1830 passed from Holyhead to Liverpool in only 23 seconds. The development of an electric telegraph made the semaphore chain obsolete in the late 1840's.

If the light at Point Lynas has a long history, it is outdone by that on the islands off the north-west corner known as the Skerries, where a beacon first burned in 1717. The lighthouse there has now recently become automated and for the first time in its history is no longer manned, being operated by remote control from Holyhead. Anglesey's most famous lighthouse, that at South Stack (37) is somewhat less venerable, as it came into operation in 1809.

# MODERN TIMES

OURISM is big business today, and Anglesey has had its flourishing small resorts since the end of the last century, some considerably expanded in the first decades of this one. Among the island's natural assets its many fine beaches stand out spectacularly, together with a coastline much more varied and attractive than one would guess from driving through the centre. This is a feature perhaps best appreciated from the sea, from where it presents a fascinating and tempting shore. Inevitably tourism is one of the island's major industries. Tourism however possesses several built-in disadvantages as an area's single industry, most notably of course its brief seasonal intensity, and Anglesey is lucky, or wise, to have diversified.

The physical contrast between the coast and the interior extends to its population and way of life. Some of the seaside towns have a distinctly English flavour; the inland villages on the other hand are intensely Welsh. Hotels, catering, and services to the tourist industry generally, employ the coastal population, and retirement and weekend cottages, along with caravan sites, form its physical environment; among the fields and down the lanes of the interior the tractor and landrover still dominate the traffic, and barns and silos and ancient farmsteads make up the characteristic built surroundings. Many fine old country houses testify to the prosperous past derived from its good land, and to its settled families.

Neither of these two variable economies — tourism and farming — or the two in combination have proved sufficient to sustain a still fair-sized population, and poverty and unemployment have from time to time, this century, posed problems. For these reasons Anglesey has energetically tried to attract modern industry, and in this it has not been without success.

That such a policy may occasionally misfire has recently been demonstrated by the closure, as obsolete, of the vastly expensive and disruptive Shell oil terminal and pipeline at Amlwch. It is possible that in due course Wylfa power station may suffer the same fate of superannuation.

Among the island's modern enterprises the Royal Air Force base at Valley now displays considerable activity, and nearby, on the outskirts of Holyhead, the Anglesey Aluminium smelting plant forms a large source of employment. This impressive complex, which took shape in 1971, has a policy of employing local people as far as possible and maintains a consciously Welsh environment. The plant turns imported alumina (a powder made from bauxite), landed at its

*Sailing on the Menai Strait near Beaumaris*

own jetty and conveyed from there by a 3,600 foot tunnel, into aluminium, which then leaves Anglesey in cast form.

All these varied, indeed contrasting, activities, and of course several others, tick away in the background of Anglesey's present social life, combining to provide a modest prosperity and with it a continuity of its independent character. With the reasonable hope of the projection of this into the future, the island now dispays as real and sturdy an identity as one would expect from a place with a history richer, more varied, and as ancient as that of any equivalent part of our nation's heritage.

# ACKNOWLEDGEMENTS

The author wishes to thank Mr Vernon Hughes, A.R.I.B.A., for help in providing information relating to the development of Holyhead; the Marquess of Anglesey for his advice and assistance in relation to the passages concerning his home, Plas Newydd; and the Gwynedd Archeological Trust for information relating to their work at Llanfaes and Newborough.

*Medieval Anglesey*, by A.D. Carr, published by the Anglesey Antiquarian Society in 1982, is a valuable source for details of the period dealt with here in chapters 4 and 5; *Copper Mountain* by John Rowlands, published by the same source in 1966, is the main authority for information on the period dealt with here in chapter 6; and *The Conwy and the Menai Ferries* by H.R. Davies, published by the University of Wales Press in 1966, is a valuable source work for some of the subjects covered in our chapter 7.

*PHOTOGRAPHS*
*All photographs by the author, except for:*
*2, 4, 12, 20, 22a, 23*
*(National Monuments Record for Wales)*
*9, 10, 13, 14, 17, 19b, 22, 28, 29, 30, 31, 32, 33, 34, 35, 36*
*(E. Emrys Jones, Bae Colwyn)*
*19*
*(Cambridge University of Air Photographs)*
*26*
*(Gwynedd Archives Service)*
*27*
*(The National Trust)*
*Front cover slide by Celtic Picture Agency.*
*Back print by kindness of Olwen Caradog Evans, Conwy.*